ENGAGE & MOBILIZE YOUR TEAM

How to get off the beaten path and get the results you need

Claire Hayek

Published by MSP Teambuilding

www.mspteambuilding.ca

ISBN : 978-1-7770991-1-4

TABLE OF CONTENTS

CHAPTER ONE

INTRODUCTION

Hello,

My name is Claire Hayek, founder of MSP Teambuilding. My team and I would like to thank you for your interest in this book.

Over the last 22 years of my career, I have had the chance to wear different hats and walk in different shoes, whether as an engineer, a team manager, project director, a singer-songwriter-producer or as a business owner to name a few. It has allowed me to understand a thing or two about human interactions in various industries from different perspectives and hierarchy levels. This hands-on knowledge was key for my team and I to develop a unique and original approach that has helped many of our customers and their employees, us included! We are truly proud to share these tools with you.

These activities have helped improve workplace interactions, despite intergenerational differences, as well as open communication and collaboration between teammates, therefore affecting employee retention and loyalty.

This book is the result of many meetings and telephone conversations we've had with employers working in different industries as well as numerous interactions with their employees. This was crucial to help us define and identify the needs at different hierarchal levels: business owners, team leaders, department heads, along with employees as a whole.

Throughout this very easy-to-read book, we will share simple and efficient tools to help you build your company culture from the bottom up, hand in hand with your employees while implementing workplace initiatives that help improve intergenerational and multicultural communication as well as team mobilization and performance.

This book was written with passion and is a gateway to our various team building programs and services based on our four pillars: Engagement, Collaboration, Performance, and Non-Monetary Recognition.

We work with companies like yours to help them improve employee engagement as well as attract and retain talent. We bring you the very best team building workshops to suit different tastes and support your people while helping your organization thrive.

Our process is simple: We assess your organization's needs and offer you specialized programs that fill gaps and build on what you're already doing well. We want to invite you - as a reader of this book - to make an appointment with us to discuss your needs and challenges by **clicking here** or by **emailing us here.** Make sure to mention that you have read this guide 'Engage & Motivate your team'.

We hope this book will serve as a stepping stone for reaching the goals you aspire to in your business, and we wish you an insightful reading. Be sure to read our customers' testimonials in the last chapter **here.**

I am looking forward to interesting and fruitful discussions with you.

Claire Hayek, MBA
President and CEO
MSP Teambuilding

CHAPTER TWO

UNDERSTANDING EMPLOYERS' AND EMPLOYEES' NEEDS

What team leaders seek above all is for their employees to perform well together and be as efficient as possible. They are looking for that perfect formula that will help them get rid of many challenges they constantly face with their teams such as lack of engagement, miscommunication, working in silos, lack of motivation or sense of belonging, lack of inspiration and creativity at the workplace, lack of trust within colleagues, intergenerational differences and the list goes on…

If we take these challenges and look at them from the employees' perspective, we realize they want the same thing as their employers. They want to be part of a happy and creative work environment, they hope to develop good relationships with their colleagues based on trust, open communication and collaboration, they want the opportunity to grow and progress within the company, and most importantly, they want to feel recognized and appreciated for their skills and talent.

Let's imagine for a second that you can succeed in overcoming these challenges at your workplace. This results in a tremendous impact on your profitability, your ability to grow your business, and your ability to attract and retain talent while building a strong, happy company culture. Wouldn't that be wonderful, right?

THIS IS POSSIBLE, and many companies have achieved this success with a lot of effort, commitment, and hard work. Many organizations spend a tremendous amount of money on employee benefits, team building activities, and events. Some hire certified professional coaches to help their leadership teams improve their managerial skills and their emotional intelligence.

Overall, these initiatives are very important for employee development yielding cyclical boosts in employee engagement- Figure 1.

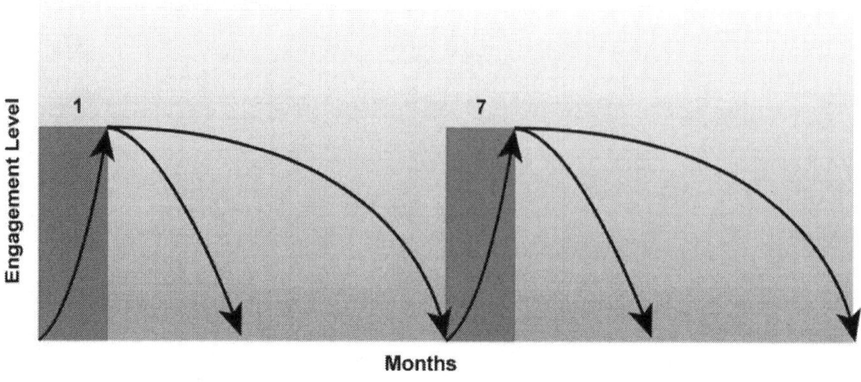

Figure 1 – Typical Employees' Engagement vs Time

However, the big question is, how can we sustain and improve employee engagement within an organization over time despite intergenerational and intercultural differences? Is it even possible?

CHAPTER THREE

THE INTERGENERATIONAL GAP

The invention of computers, the internet, and smartphones has been great in many ways. For one thing, information is right at our fingertips. If we need an answer to a question, all we have to do is google it. Is there something we want to automate in our lives? Well, there's an app for that.

However, all these improvements have a downside. The downside is that new generations are lacking soft skills[1], and this may impact how well your team members can effectively interact, communicate, and collaborate together. We often associate this generational gap between millennials and older generations.

Before we go any further, here's how the generations are usually defined[2]:

- The Silent Generation: Born 1928-1945
- Baby Boomers: Born 1946-1964
- Generation X: Born 1965-1980

- Millennials or Generation Y: Born 1981-1996
- Post-Millennials or Generation Z: Born 1997-Present

While millennials have truly mastered hard skills, the heavy use of technology has left a gap in the soft skills department, especially in face- to-face communication, talking on the phone, and sending emails. These necessary skills have been replaced with direct messaging, social media sized information snippets, and disappearing images, to name a few.

According to a recent McKinsey study[3], 40 % of employers said they have difficulty filling vacancies because younger workers lack soft skills such as communication, teamwork, and punctuality.

On the other hand, a 2018 Deloitte millennial survey[4] says millennials are increasingly looking to their employers to give them the skills they need to succeed. They are especially interested in building interpersonal skills, confidence, and ethical behavior.

For instance, if we focus on millennials, we can understand why they think and behave the way they do and how this may affect their interactions at the workplace.

They grew up in the technological age and are often judged for using their phones frequently even though that trend has now caught on to most generations. The only difference is that older generations have experienced life without cell phones and therefore had good practice with direct, face-to-face communication.

Millennials' vision of the world is different, which affects their work ethics and motivation. They want to feel valued and see value in their work. They are attracted to organizations that allow them to manifest their beliefs and make a difference by helping others. They want to be inspired by the company culture and mission.

Older generations have strong work ethics, as they believe you need to work hard to earn your respect or move up the ladder. Millennials, for instance, tend to be labeled as entitled and arrogant. Their discontentment towards a closed-up and rigid hierarchal organizations may be mistaken for self-confidence. They would rather take initiative, do things their own way, and learn from their mistakes as opposed to turning to experienced colleagues for guidance. This behavior is understandable since instant gratification is their best friend. Older generations had to get out of the house and visit a library to have access to the information they needed.

These behaviors and anchored values that differ from one generation to the other often create barriers to communication at the workplace. This is why developing employees' emotional intelligence[5] (EQ) and openness is key to bridging the intergenerational gap. As a matter of fact, some researchers6 have shared data showing that emotional intelligence makes up 75% of our intelligence compared to only 25% for our rational intelligence associated with the intelligence quotient (IQ).

An individual's EQ has been shown to predict success better than one's IQ. Emotional intelligence allows employees to succeed better in business and personal relationships, have a better focus on work with clear thoughts, as well as tremendously help in coping with different types of situations.

Of course, the same applies to intercultural differences. For those of you who are avid travelers, you can agree that visiting different countries or continents has allowed you to develop your ability to understand how certain human behaviors are directly related to one's culture and traditions. Travel has also shown to boost one's EQ due to our tendency to socialize a bit more when we travel. We learn to listen more and interrupt less.

The good news is emotional intelligence can be taught, developed, and improved, therefore, affecting a team's EQ and ability to communicate efficiently. Consequently, it will positively affect how team members interact, will help bridge the intergenerational gap, and increase team performance.

CHAPTER FOUR

THE BEATEN PATH- WHAT MOST ORGANIZATIONS DO

There are many methods and tools available when it comes to boosting employee engagement as well as mobilizing teams. As long as it gets you the results you need, there is no right or wrong.

Let's take a look at what most organizations do.

The following is a simplified summary of some typical approaches to team engagement that we have often observed. Please note this may not necessarily cover all approaches available out there, what you and your organization may have tried in the past, or what your organization is doing at the present moment.

1. For small teams:

- Dedicate a budget for social activities at the workplace
- Form a social club with or without employee contribution, or
- Assign the task to the:
  - Human Resources (HR) personnel
  - Communication and Marketing department
  - Event planning team
  - Team leader or management
- Plan one to three activities a year. This can include a summer barbecue, a volunteering event to give back to the community, an employee recognition gala, a team building activity, a meeting retreat, a Christmas party, etc.
- Little to no activities planned in between
- Repeat

2. For leadership teams

- Dedicate a budget for leadership training and advancement
- Assign the task to the:
    - Human Resources (HR) personnel
    - Communication and Marketing department
    - Event planning team
    - Team leader or management
- Typically plan one or two meetings a year in a retreat type of setting
- Hire a professional coach or highly qualified and certified professionals to teach your team about or address specific needs, such as how to improve managerial skills, how to be an authentic leader, etc.
- Little to no activities planned in between
- Repeat

3. For the whole organization

- Assign a budget for one or two mobilizing initiatives or team building activities across all regions or branches.

- The goal is geared towards building or reinforcing company culture, mission, and values and getting to know your colleagues across regions/branches.
- Assign the task to the:
    - Human Resources (HR) personnel
    - Communication and Marketing department
    - Event planning team
- Little to no activities planned in between
- Repeat

Of course, some organizations may also choose to adopt a combination of the above. Again, there is no right or wrong way here. In fact, some organizations have succeeded in finding their own unique combination to suit their specific needs.

No matter what combination you have tried, what is often overlooked by many organizations is the ability of their approach to sustain employee engagement and motivation over long periods of time. Therefore, the key is to maintain and slowly build engagement for long-term results as opposed to achieving a yo-yo effect with high and low engagement. This steadily rising curve is crucial, so all the time, effort, and money spent on these activities yield a positive return over time. Some may say that this is pure wishful thinking, but contrary to popular belief, this is possible.

CHAPTER FIVE

THE YO-YO EFFECT

The three approaches listed in the previous chapter were used to illustrate what is typically done when it comes to boosting employee engagement. Let's take a look at the expected outcome of these methods and their effect on the organization and employees over time.

1- During and shortly after the activity

- A huge motivational boost for all
- Feeling inspired and connected to colleagues
- Teams are empowered
- Communication is fluid and collaboration is at its best
- A great sense of pride and belonging to the organization

2- Post-activity (weeks or some months later in rare cases)

- It's business as usual with a bit more enthusiasm
- Good team spirit
- Workload is prominent, but employees feel motivated and engaged
- Good performance throughout and people are generally getting along
- There's still some talk about the activity and teams recapitulate the amazing bonding experience they shared together

3- 'Post' post-activity (many months later)

- It's still business as usual with less enthusiasm towards teammates
- Stress is induced from a heavy workload or when personal life weighs in
- The ability to communicate together is not at its best
- The energy level is decreasing as well as personal motivation
- Frustration is building up

- The strong memories everyone shared together are either long gone or have slowly faded to the background
- Employees may feel depressed or disconnected from their job

4- **Organizations plan a new activity to boost motivation and engagement**
5- **Repeat.**

This yo-yo effect illustrated in figure 1 in chapter 2 depicts very well the reality of most organizations when it comes to team mobilization. This is to be expected, because the impact of stress over time is inevitable, and as humans, we have our limits. Some can deal with it better than others and keep their stress level under control, but this, unfortunately, doesn't apply to everyone.

The same holds true when it comes to motivation. Keeping everyone motivated at the same level is literally impossible, and that's a fact. Individual motivations are best analyzed and explained by a psychometric test7. The bottom line is that this yo-yo effect can tremendously impact team engagement and motivation, and consequently, it can turn into a domino effect, upsetting employee performance and business profitability.

Understanding and recognizing the existence of this yo-yo effect is the first step to avoiding it altogether. The root cause of the problem is the fact that organizations are caught in a reactive approach to team mobilization as opposed to a proactive one. The focus should be on minimizing or eliminating the drop in engagement before it even has a chance to begin.

CHAPTER SIX

OFF-THE-BEATEN PATH- WHAT ORGANIZATIONS SHOULD DO

No matter which department you work for in an organization, who you report to, or who reports to you, productivity and profitability are key for success and growth. Simply put, when a business depends on employee performance, an investment of time, energy, and money must be allocated to:

- Attracting and retaining talent
- Increasing employee productivity and motivation
- Improving communication and collaboration within teams
- Building a strong, happy company culture
- Developing your corporate social responsibility (CSR)
- Etc.

What we usually see are organizations focusing on one or two aspects to reach their goal. Let's take the Tech industry as an example. We have observed that attracting and retaining talent is their main focus. These specialized employees, typically programmers and developers, amongst others, are not only scarce but are also very difficult to retain due to the industry's high demand and increasingly competitive salaries and benefits. The same is applicable in the engineering consultancy industry and many other industries.

Some companies focus on improving their CSR and company culture to attract and retain talent. Even when they succeed, it doesn't guarantee their teams will be productive, engaged, and collaborative. The point here is that organizations nowadays are left with no choice but to improve their processes at all levels to keep their employees engaged, productive, and happy. It is simply a full-time job when you think of it. This necessity gave rise to new specialized job positions in organizations, such as Team Builders, Talent Acquisition Managers, Engagement and Culture Directors, People Culture Managers, CSR managers, and others.

As previously mentioned, the key is to work towards developing and building engagement in small increments but in a consistent upward manner. I will get straight to the point and tell you how this can be achieved efficiently on a budget. The following are the steps to get you the results you need.

1. Assess and measure

Assessing and understanding your employee needs is crucial because it defines your starting point. Measuring your team's engagement level is part of this step, and it provides a benchmark for improvement. If you don't know where you rank, how can you possibly know whether or not your approach is working and if your results are improving? For this, I recommend a short, five- question survey sent to your team members to assess and measure team spirit. It is important for the survey to be anonymous i.e., a survey that keeps respondents' identities private. This will encourage survey participation, and you'll receive honest responses that can help you better evaluate the present mood.

Here are some of the questions we use in our surveys at MSP Teambuilding. We provide this survey to our customers before our team building workshops to measure and assess their current engagement level. The questions in Italic are generic but are designed to be revised to fit the context you are in. For example, if you're assessing your team, you can change the phrasing of the question, so it's more specific to your team as opposed to the 'organization' as a whole. I included a bit more information on each question to give you more insight on the approach:

1- **Culture**: *On a scale from 0-10, how likely are you to recommend your organization as a good place to work?*

   This question is aimed to measure the employee net promoter score, eNPS[8]. It's a simple way to assess what employees like and don't like about your organization and a great way to indirectly measure employee engagement.

2- **Work environment**: *Do you feel like your work environment reflects your organizational culture?*

This is important to know. For instance, if a company claims that it encourages employees to be innovative but doesn't allow them to share their ideas openly, they may feel a disconnect between the company environment and its culture.

3- **Recognition**: *Do you feel recognized and valued by your organization (or your supervisor/team leader/superior)?*

This question helps define the level of recognition an employee feels more importantly on a non-monetary level.

4- **Relationship with manager**: *Do you feel like you can trust your manager?*

This question helps shed some light on the trust level as well as communication and collaboration between employees and their superior.

5- **Relationship with colleagues**: *Do you and your colleagues collaborate well together?*

Feeling included is important in a team setting. This question measures where you stand when it comes to inclusion and collaboration so you can work towards improving it.

Another effective way to understand your strengths and weaknesses as a team is to invest in a psychometric analysis of your group. Team profile assessments are a great way to dive deeply into the personality of your whole team, department, or organization. The purpose is to give you more information and insights about your team as a whole.

A team profile places everyone's personalities onto one grid and shows you which traits are dominant within your team. When you combine the profiles into a global one, you will be able to see which traits are predominant, where their strengths come from, and what it will take to make them exceptional. This helps shed more light on the best way to train, motivate, lead, and engage your people.

Many providers offer this service, so don't be afraid to ask your network for recommendations. It would be my pleasure to share mine with you, please don't hesitate to ask.

2. The cyclical boost

Once you have assessed your team's general mood, start the process with a team building activity to give it the boost it needs. For instance, if you identify that trust and collaboration is an issue amongst your group, then choose an activity that will challenge your team members and leave them no choice but to collaborate. Let me elaborate on this a bit more.

On many occasions, I have observed that participants tend to work together and collaborate better when faced with a team building activity that puts them completely out of their comfort zone. It's human nature to work together and collaborate when faced with the unknown or the inconceivable task. It takes a lot of courage to dive in; therefore, it is much easier to do so as a team than on your own. Our survival instincts kick in, and we automatically work together to overcome the challenge at hand. This is a known fact, and it is often observed in nature when animals work together to hunt their prey.

What is extremely important here is to focus on the team strength and not to single out 'the fittest' or 'the smartest' or the most 'talented.' It is empirical for all team members to feel that they are at the same level with no hierarchy involved. Creative team building activities, such as music, visual arts, audiovisual and others, are a great fit to boost team collaboration and communication.

The reason for this is that although we all have a creative gene in us, most people do not necessarily invest in developing and exploring their inner artist because it is a scary path to follow. People often portray artists as being extravagant or living on a different planet or in a parallel universe. Arts and music are unknown territories for most of us; we enjoy it, but we do not necessarily want to wear the artist hat. This is exactly why team building workshops featuring arts and music are the best platforms for instant collaboration. It is much easier for a team to become the artist as opposed to one team member taking front and center stage.

The best part is that your team will walk away feeling empowered and motivated because they would live a unique experience, and as a group, they will succeed in creating a piece of art they never thought they were capable of achieving. Some of these creative workshops also provide a memento to part with that will extend the effect of this exceptional moment.

An example would be a beautiful art piece created by your team that you can exhibit at your office as a reminder of your team collaboration or a recording of a song you wrote and interpreted together to highlight your mission and values as an organization. The song makes for a great memento that can be played at your next event and will be sure to bring back some laughter. These are two examples of powerful activities that help create strong, positive emotions that can be easily etched in your employees' memories.

At this stage, no matter what activity you end up choosing, aim for one that will maximize your return on investment by making sure it will sustain its effectiveness for at least a month.

Finally, a post-activity survey should be shared with your team to measure the direct impact of the activity. Therefore, measuring the before and after will help you evaluate your progress. I strongly suggest that the survey questions are developed in the same context as the previous one with different phrasing. I would be happy to share our surveys with you if needed.

3. Anticipate the cyclical drop

The motivation and excitement will inevitably drop with time; therefore, you must anticipate it to keep the momentum of a continuously increasing team engagement. This can be done by sharing another team survey a month or two post activity to re-assess everyone's morale and catch the curve as it starts to ease its way back down.

Some might feel that this is far too many surveys sent in a short period of time, therefore, negatively affecting survey participation and I agree with you on that. However, there are many effective methods to increase your survey response rate. Here are a few I'd like to share:

- **Express your appreciation for their participation**- Tell them that you want to know what they think and that you value their opinion
- **Keep it short**- It should take a maximum of 5 minutes for someone to complete your survey
- **Provide incentives**- At this stage of the process (i.e. 3rd survey), discounts, gift cards and raffles are very effective in increasing response rates. I recommend using this once or twice and not making a habit of it. Also, make sure your incentives appeal to everyone.

If the idea of sending a third survey doesn't interest you, you can safely anticipate some sort of drop in motivation roughly a month later. All good things must come to an end, right? So now what do we do? How can we sustain enthusiasm and motivation when our team is stressed, overworked, and tired?

4. Keep up the momentum

Here's the big secret revealed. Actually, it is the simple solutions that are often overlooked and the most effective, and it is no exception here. Team building activities planned two or three times a year are great but cannot be effective on their own. You need to keep up that team spirit by feeding it regularly. Some have actually made it a monthly and even a bi-weekly habit, yes, every two weeks. What exactly am I referring to?

I am talking about organizing recurring in-house team building activities at little to no cost to your organization. This will go a long way to maximizing the effectiveness of the cyclical boosts provided by outsourced team building workshops. The ultimate goal here is to build durable boosts to not only stop that inevitable drop in engagement but also to keep increasing it in small increments, on a monthly basis, in a simple, stable and predictable way, as illustrated in figure 2. You might be telling yourself that you already do that with your existing social club. What I'm suggesting here is far different. Let me explain.

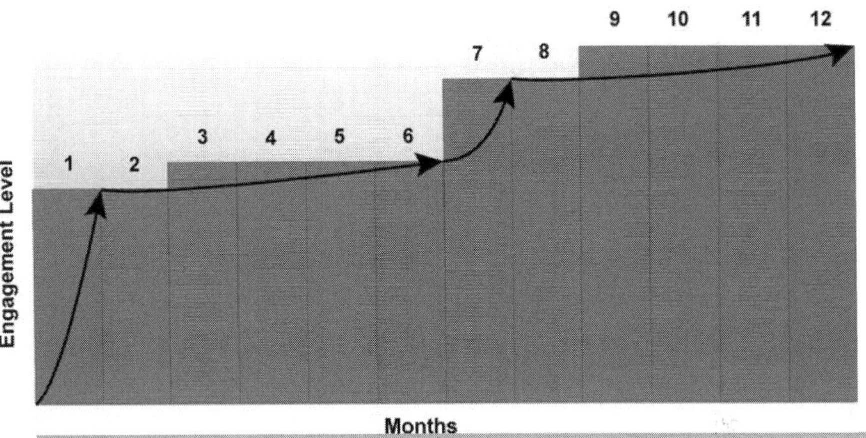

Figure 2 - Consistent Employees' Engagement vs Time

Typically, sports and social clubs are created and run by a group of employees. They are funded by employers which is a great way to encourage employees' initiatives and leadership. One of the limitations of these committees is the fact that they attract specific types of personalities as leading members: outgoing, natural leaders, creative, ease with event planning, social butterflies, etc. Therefore, it doesn't necessarily involve your whole team including employees that don't like to be in the spotlight, introverts, or the hidden talents waiting to be discovered.

Another important shortcoming of social clubs is that activities are chosen with the main goal to please co-workers as a whole and not necessarily focus on developing your team skills and instilling team engagement. These clubs cannot be blamed for that because it is very difficult as it is to satisfy everyone with one social activity. We, therefore, don't leave them much of a choice but to go with the most popular and most fun activity for all. I completely sympathize with social clubs as I was part of many of them and let me tell you that it was not an easy task.

Again, this is in no way belittling the effectiveness of sports and social clubs. In fact, the latter has proven to build employee motivation and support employees' emotional and physical wellbeing. However, their effectiveness can also be categorized as cyclical.

The approach I am suggesting works well at all levels if and only if certain steps are followed and respected.

CHAPTER SEVEN

THE GRASSROOTS APPROACH-BUILD IT FROM THE BOTTOM UP

We often see companies struggle with employee participation when it comes to organized activities, such as company barbeques, volunteering activities, team building activities, or others. This is especially observed in organizations lacking company culture due to reasons such as high employee turnover rate, hierarchal leadership, oppressive management, etc. However, even the companies that rank high in company culture may struggle to keep their employees engaged. We have simply found that when you provide opportunities for your employees to take initiative and shine, they step up. The grassroots approach suggested here does exactly that.

Empowering employees from the bottom up creates a work environment where creativity is valued. It also allows team leaders to get to know their teams in a different way and restructure meetings to encourage collaboration. Here are the six essential steps to help you succeed in this process:

1. **Define your needs** – Choose three to five skills you would like to develop as a team over the next twelve months. Here are a few examples:
    a. Collaboration
    b. Communication
    c. Creativity
    d. Motivation
    e. Critical thinking
    f. Accountability
2. **Choose a recurring timeslot and a place** – This is essential because it will help increase participation. Ideally, you should choose a day of the week when you know your team is at the office and will be available for an hour or two. Most of our customers elect to do these activities later in the week when a break is mostly needed. Fridays at noon or Friday afternoons are the most popular. Some choose the second or the last Friday of the month as the recurring date, which simplifies the whole process, and they plan the activity in the office cafeteria or common area.

3. **Make it an event!** – Assign a budget for the activity to include food and drinks. This simple reward goes a long way, and you don't have to go overboard. If you're on a tight budget, you can offer them drinks and/ or dessert or simply make it a potluck. The latter is an excellent way to increase participation and a great intercultural icebreaker for all.

   Some organizations provide food, drinks, a sound system with music playing in the background to set the mood, foosball tables, pool tables, dartboards, etc. Others give the recurring event a theme to inspire positivity, strength, and a sense of belonging or just to make it fun. Use your imagination and respect your budget, so this can be sustained during the whole year. Avoid raising the bar too high. Instead, keep it simple and efficient.

4. **Activity Facilitation** – Your one to two-hour activity now has a date, time, and place. It also has a theme that corresponds to one of your needs. I will share with you some examples of activities in the next chapter, but most importantly, let's discuss how the activity should be facilitated.

The best way to encourage engagement and motivation is to post a sign- up sheet in a common area that is accessible to everyone. The idea is to encourage employees to team up as a group of three or more and take the initiative to host the activity together. What we found works best is to have the activities facilitated by a group of different employees every month. This avoids having the same people hosting the activities over and over again. Below is an example of a sign-up sheet for your reference.

If you're a large group such as 100 employees or more, you can have two activities per event with two facilitation groups. If you're a large organization, you can organize these activities per department and focus on the outsourced team building workshops for all your employees. This method can be easily adapted and fine-tuned to suit your company size.

	Date	Theme	Activity	Facilitators	Potluck
1	...	Collaboration	Outsourced	n/a	N
2	...	Leadership			Y
3		Communication			N
4		Creativity			Y
5		Accountability			N
6		Emotional Intelligence	Outsourced	n/a	N
7		Critical Thinking			N
8		Intrapreneurship			Y
9		Motivation			N
10		CSR			N
11		Innovation			Y
12		Volunteering	Outsourced	n/a	N

Figure 3- Activities' Facilitation Sign-up Sheet Example

5. **What's your incentive?** – Steps 1 to 4 above can only work if you clearly communicate the goal of this initiative and if you assign a common, selfless incentive to make it a success.

For instance, you can set a dollar amount to be donated to a charity based on activity participation or conditional to all employees signing up as a facilitator at least once throughout the year. Another incentive could be to link participation to employee yearly evaluations for example, under 'Attitude/Initiative/Teamwork,' so on and so forth. The incentive you choose needs to be non-monetary in nature to avoid 'buying' your team participation.

Finally, if all incentives fail, which is less likely but nevertheless a possibility, you might need to take a different approach. In this case, employees should be asked to form their own groups and sign up to facilitate an activity by a certain deadline, usually within a month. The remaining employees that failed to sign-up by that deadline will automatically be assigned to a facilitation group at a specific date. Therefore, if for any reason, you choose not to take initiative to sign-up your own team members, you will be assigned to a random team.

The idea here is to make sure everyone participates in one way or another. Again, this is strictly in order to avoid the same group filling in and facilitating for others which would end up resembling a 'social club' type of committee.

Remember, the goal is to gradually instill a culture of collaboration and engagement within teams using these activities as a tool to do so. It is certainly not about forcing people into it but simply supporting them and giving them a hand in the process.

6. **Persistence** – It is not only important to properly launch this initiative, but it is also important to make sure to stick with it regardless of day-to-day highs and lows, busy and slow months. If a one-hour activity monthly is too difficult to sustain then make it a bi-monthly, two-hour activity instead. Keeping the momentum is key to mobilizing your team and sustaining engagement.

   There will be periods during the year where people are feeling a bit overwhelmed. That is normal but it's important for you to stay agile and not to drop the ball. If no one from your team is willing to facilitate in a specific month, you can show your support and hire outside team building facilitators to host the activity during that tough time period, or you can choose to move up your outsourced team building activity and fill in the gap by giving the workplace a motivational boost.

   Not hosting the event and dropping the ball can send a subtle message that you are not living up to your end of the deal. This grassroots approach does involve upper management as a solid support to this initiative. Do your absolute best to keep that momentum and mix it up to avoid routine.

In the following chapter, I will share with you easy tools and examples of activities your team can lead and facilitate.

CHAPTER EIGHT

SIMPLE TOOLS TO DEVELOP TEAM ENGAGEMENT

To recapitulate, it is imperative to organize recurring in-house team building activities that add great value to employee engagement on a little to no- cost basis. These activities prolongate the effectiveness of the cyclical boosts provided by outsourced team building workshops and help increase engagement in small increments in a steady manner.

There is a tremendous number of team building activities that can be easily organized and facilitated in-house that can be found on the internet. The possibilities are endless. I will now share simple activities that are highly effective and fun in a team setting. I chose to focus these tools around four pillars that are, from my experience, crucial to team mobilization and engagement. I call them the four Cs: Communication, Collaboration, Creativity, and Critical thinking.

The following games will take approximately 20-30 minutes to complete. The facilitators will need 5 minutes to brief participants and set-up, 10-20 minutes to complete the challenge and another 5 minutes to review and debrief the activity. Facilitators need to be prepared to coach the activity from beginning to end, including the review and debrief. The latter is crucial as this is the time when all team members will share their views on the activity and what they learned or liked about it. It also helps improve team emotional intelligence by learning to listen to one another and express emotions openly.

Some suggested review questions are:

- What was the most challenging aspect of the activity for you?
- What did you enjoy about the activity?
- What did you learn about yourself or your colleagues?
- How well did you work as a team?
- How could you have improved?
- How can this experience be applied in your day-to-day tasks?

Finally, the games will be far more effective if certain rules are made clear right from the start, such as:

- Hierarchy and titles are left at the door. All participants are brought to the same level as one entity throughout the activity;
- A good playful team spirit and an open mind are encouraged throughout the duration of the activity;
- Judgment, disrespect and negative criticism will not be tolerated and can disqualify a team;
- Team members are selected by facilitators prior to starting the activity and selections are not negotiable;
- Facilitators will choose team members to:
    - Encourage interaction between employees that don't know each other well or that rarely communicate together;
    - Encourage gender, age, and cultural diversity.
- Most important rule is to remember that this is just a game, so have fun and enjoy it!

A- Communication- Magic Cane

The magic cane or helium stick game is a simple activity to encourage team communication while facing a common challenge. First, start by dividing participants into groups of 8 to 12 or 6 to 14. Try to keep teams in even numbers.

Once the groups are identified, the challenge is for each team to slowly lower a helium stick to the ground without dropping it using their index fingers. A helium stick is a thin, light-weight rod that can be fabricated in-house by attaching straws together, or you can buy a thin, light-weight bamboo cane from the dollar store. This may sound like a simple task, but it is quite challenging. It can actually become incredibly frustrating and funny for all involved.

Each group must create two lines on each side and face each other. The facilitators introduce the cane to each group. With the stick lying horizontally in the middle, have each person put their index finger underneath it. Everyone's index fingers must be in contact with the stick. Explain that the challenge is to lower the cane to the ground.

The rule is that everybody's index fingers must remain in contact with the cane at all times. Pinching or grabbing the stick is not permitted – it must rest on top of fingers only.

Reiterate to the group that if anyone's finger is caught not touching the cane, the challenge will be restarted. (Some may try to find a loophole in the rules by starting on their knees.)

Every person is needed to complete the task, so members must work together and communicate. This reinforces the idea that everyone is equally important, valuable, and necessary for the team to succeed.

B- Collaboration- Follow the leader

This activity can involve a group from 10 up to 80 participants. It will require the whole team to work together as one. A secret leader will make simple movements that the entire group will quickly mimic. One guesser will be left in the middle of the group to determine who the leader is. This quick activity is easy to facilitate and is a great way to get your team up and moving. It can be done indoors or outdoors.

I strongly suggest that the secret guesser and leader are determined on the spot by a random name draw. You need to first start by drawing the name of the guesser. He or she is then asked to leave the room while you draw the name of the leader. You can then assemble the group in a circle and have everyone practice briefly before the guesser returns.

Once the guesser returns, have him or her stand in the middle of the circle, then you can signal the group to start when ready. The key is for participants to avoid any eye contact with the leader as they mimic his or her moves; otherwise, they will easily give it away. The guesser can start guessing who the leader is the moment the movements begin. You can repeat the process by changing the guesser and leader once the guesser figures out who the leader is. You can also time each guesser to figure out who guesses in the shortest time.

The main focus of this game is team collaboration, but it also improves non- verbal communication, trust, and team cohesion. It's a fun and simple activity that can effectively improve team engagement.

C- Creativity- Arts & Craft for Charity

This activity can involve a group from 10 up to 80 participants. It will require splitting everyone into teams of five to 10 members. For instance, if you have 80 participants, you can work with ten teams. The goal of this game is to have each team create crafts that will be donated to a children's center, a charitable cause, or the elderly.

Facilitators need to choose the theme of the crafts, depending on who you would like to donate it to. Craft stations, including tools, can then be set-up. Each team is then asked to pick their craft activity from a jar and sit at the assigned craft station. Once all teams are assigned to their stations, each will have 30 minutes to create crafts worthy of a donation to a charitable cause. Provide basic instructions on how to create each craft and leave the rest to the team's imagination.

This is a great activity to put your team creativity to work and watch your colleagues unveil their inner artist. Here are some examples of easy crafts you can make that can be of great use to donate to a charitable cause. You can do a search to get all the details needed to make them.

- Create handmade stationery
- Create a mini desk organizer
- Make grippy socks
- Back-to-School Crafts with decorative Tape

D- Critical Thinking- This is better than that

Facilitators bring in four objects (or multiple sets of four objects) of the same type (e.g. four different sets of mittens, four different coffee mugs). They write up a conversational scenario for each set that outlines what the perfect item would be, in the order of preference. While none of the four objects of these sets is an exact match, each have qualities that reflect that perfect list.

Facilitators can then read this scenario to the different groups, and instruct them to order the objects from best fit to worst fit. You can give teams 10-15 minutes to deliberate and finish the task. This can be repeated with a different set of objects as needed. When all sets are done, have team members of each group explain why they ordered the objects that way.

The key to this exercise is to make the scenario complex enough that it isn't immediately obvious which objects are best. It, therefore, helps teams analyze facts to form a judgment and think critically individually and as a team. The following skills are then applied:

- Observation
- Analysis
- Interpretation
- Reflection
- Evaluation
- Inference
- Explanation
- Problem-solving and
- Decision making

The activity ends with the facilitators acting as a jury and deciding who the winners are for each set of objects and why. This makes for an interesting discussion and debrief between the facilitators and the different teams. You can choose to ask everyone which skills of the critical thinking process were the easiest and which ones were the hardest for them.

This exercise gives great insight into how teams work together when faced with problem-solving and helps them identify their strong skills and the ones they need to develop further.

Photos of different team building games facilitated with intergenerational teams

Photos of different team building games facilitated with intergenerational teams (cont'd)

CHAPTER NINE

THE IMPORTANCE OF CSR[9] IN TEAM MOBILIZATION

I'm sure you've heard that Corporate Social Responsibility (CSR) within an organization is good for business because these efforts boost profits and improve a company's image as well as its customer relations. These are not the only reasons why CSR is important in our modern age. CSR is also key to boosting employee relations.

In a 2012 paper in the "Journal of Management," industrial-organizational psychologists Herman Aguinis and Ante Glavas provided a detailed review of CSR effects on employees within an organization, and the results were astounding. As Bob Stiller, founder of Green Mountain Coffee Roasters, has said, "I've learned that people are motivated and more willing to go the extra mile to make the company successful when there's a higher good associated with it. It's no longer just a job. Work becomes meaningful, and this makes us more competitive."

CSR encourages collaboration[10] between colleagues as well as the organization and inspires closer and better relationships throughout[11]. Corporate Social Responsibility activities at the workplace motivate teams to make a difference in their community and give them a platform to make the world a better place. A great stress-relief, these activities boost team morale and provide a high sense of wellbeing.

Here are some interesting facts drawn from recent studies about CSR in relation to employees' retention and engagement:

- There is a 50% reduction in employee turnover when employees are engaged in CSR programs[12]
- 75% of millennials say they would take a pay cut to work for a responsible company[13]

Therefore, when the subject of team mobilization and engagement comes up, we can no longer ignore the importance of CSR and its impact on it. CSR helps build company loyalty. Social and environmental responsibility benefits society, employees are engaged in the work they're doing, productivity goes up, and public perception is more positive. Therefore, CSR activities are a great way to motivate your team while giving back to your community and building a positive ethical company culture and image. Everyone wins!

Here are five examples of CSR activities you can take on that are simple and highly effective:

1- **Volunteering** as a team for a cause or to give back to your community
2- **Decorating** your workspace with plants or moss or building a vegetation wall. This has many benefits, such as reducing stress, reducing fatigue, and improving your office air quality.
3- **Team meditation or yoga** to inspire better health and wellbeing. When done consistently, meditation reduces stress, improves focus, and relaxes the body and mind. As a result, meditation can improve business productivity.
4- **Laughter yoga** as a team mood booster. When done regularly, it can help teach your team to keep a positive mental state when dealing with difficult situations. In addition, it will help your team connect more easily and can improve relationships.

5- **Social intrapreneurship initiatives** to encourage employees to take on their own social initiative as intrapreneurs[14]. Participating employees present an initiative to create a good social or environmental impact by giving back to their community or helping a charitable cause, and moving the company's mission forward. Giving employees this opportunity encourages engagement at the workplace and helps identify natural leaders within your team.

These little steps can get you on the right path. CSR efforts have become more and more prominent to attract talent. For many job candidates, CSR programs that companies have in place are highly considered when looking at a new job. By increasing these efforts and implementing CSR activities, you'll attract and retain the best talent, increase employee engagement and productivity, and build company culture and improve company image.

CHAPTER TEN

CONCLUSION

I truly hope this book has given you insight on how to tackle team engagement and mobilization simply and effectively in order to achieve solid results that will be sustainable in time. The tools I share in this book are based on an approach that has proven to be effective for many different industries. Also, it provides the necessary explanation to carry out different monthly activities with your team in an independent manner.

Our clients are, like many organizations, looking for solutions to tackle the challenges they face with their teams at the workplace. We find that planning ahead is the best way to get the results you need. That is why my team and I have put together tailored packages built on four strong pillars: engagement, collaboration, performance, and non-monetary recognition.

These packages are designed to boost and sustain team engagement and motivation all year long and can include:

- Team building programs and surveys
- Assistance in facilitating team building games at the workplace
- Team psychometric analysis to target specific activities
- Certified coaches for specific needs identified within your organization

I encourage you to take on this initiative and transform your team into a fireball of productivity and engagement. It may seem hard at first but it surely will empower and drive you towards a happy and collaborative workplace culture.

I'm concluding this book with customer testimonials as an example of results you can achieve when the right tools are used in the process.

I look forward to when our paths cross, and I say 'see you soon'!

Claire Hayek

Find us on social media

CUSTOMER TESTIMONIALS

'Very powerful team building exercise, that demonstrates without any doubt how teams can collaborate better and greatly improve their performance. The activity is fun, pleasant, and uplifting- very well done!'- **Jason Taylor, Director**

'We've approached MSP Teambuilding to help create a group activity that would allow many of our team members to get to know each other better. The activity allowed our group to bond together in an hour and a half. The people who came out of the room were not the same people who had entered it. I highly recommend the activity for those who want to mobilize their team, it's excellent' - **Martin Lavoie, Office Director**

'It was a pleasure working with Claire and her team at MSP Teambuilding. Both professional and dynamic, Claire was able to guide us in the process of recording a song, all together. An energizing activity that fits very well with the EMBA McGill-HEC Montréal collaboration module ... even with 45 people!' - **Alain Gosselin, Director**

'It's a creative and daring exercise of collaboration that brings teams together.'- **Michel Bundock, CEO**

'Claire and her entire team helped us live a wonderful moment together. The activity was around collaboration and it made us realize the advantages of a collaborating team. I highly recommend MSP Teambuilding services.' **-Gerard Mulimbi, Managing Director**

'I tremendously appreciated the experience with MSP Teambuilding. It was such a memorable moment for us as a team and Claire was incredible!' **–Livia Arrigoni, Director**

'Thanks again to all of you for this fun and innovative activity that has allowed us to have a very positive experience with our team. It made great discoveries and achievements possible as a group' **– Anick Labrosse- Chief of Administrative Services, CIT & CMO**

'We really enjoyed it. The activity was well done and well planned. We accomplished something that I believe really brought us together!' **- Livio Di Francesco, Vice President & General Manager**

'Thank you, Claire and MSP Teambuilding team, for the fantastic activity. It was such a wonderful moment where the cohort just became one thanks to you, your team and your music. Keep up the great work and inspiration!' **–Ignace Mouzannar, Director of Engineering**

'Singing a song may seem trivial, but when you are asked to rewrite the lyrics with strong keywords that have a deep meaning for us as a team and then interpret the song together with your colleagues, the result is simply incredible. What a great collaboration exercise! Thanks to Claire Hayek and all her team at MSP Teambuilding for this great gift.' **- Louis Coulombe, Business Lawyer/ Strategic Counsel**

'MSP Teambuilding brought a unique touch of originality to our conference by allowing participants to go beyond themselves' **– Edouard Biot, President & CEO**

ENDNOTES

1 Personal attributes that enable someone to interact effectively and harmoniously with other people

2 Pew Research Center- 2018

3 McKinsey Global Institute- Technology, jobs, and the future of work, May 2017 | Executive Briefing

4 2018 Deloitte Millennial Survey- Millennials disappointed in business, unprepared for Industry 4.0

5 Goleman- Emotional Intelligence (EQ) is defined as the ability to identify, assess, and control one's own emotions, the emotions of others, and that of groups.

6 Daniel Goleman- Emotional Intelligence: Why It Can Matter More Than IQ, 2005

7 Psychometric tests are a standard and scientific method used to measure individuals' mental capabilities and behavioural style. Psychometric tests are designed to measure candidates' suitability for a role based on the required personality characteristics and aptitude (or cognitive abilities).

8 eNPS stands for employee Net Promoter Score and is a way for organizations to measure employee loyalty- officevibe.com

9 Corporate social responsibility is a type of international private business self- regulation that aims to contribute to societal goals of a philanthropic, activist, or charitable nature or by engage in or support volunteering or ethically-oriented practices.

10 Modeling Corporate Citizenship and Its Relationship with Organizational Citizenship Behaviors- Journal of business ethics, volume 95, issue 3.

11 How Does Doing Good Matter?: Effects of Corporate Citizenship on Employees- Journal of Corporate Citizenship; Winter 2009, Issue 36.

12 Project ROI: report- Defining the competitive and financial advantages of corporate responsibility and sustainability.

13 2016 Cone communications employee engagement study

14 Employees who develop an innovative idea or project within a company

INDEX

G

H

I

M

N

O

P

R

S

Made in the USA
Columbia, SC
24 July 2023

20797613R00041